ZERO TO HERO

GET YOUR MIND *to* MILITARY GRADE PERFORMANCE *to* TAKE ACTION
with SPEED, CERTAINITY, *and* EASE

FOR TODAY'S BUSINESS OWNERS, CORPORATES, AND DECISION MAKERS...

ZERO TO HERO

GET YOUR MIND *to* **MILITARY GRADE PERFORMANCE** *to* **TAKE ACTION** *with* **SPEED, CERTAINITY,** *and* **EASE**

RAKESH ARYA

Published Internationally by

Pendown Press

Powered by Gullybaba

PENDOWN PRESS
Powered by Gullybaba Publishing House Pvt. Ltd.,
An ISO 9001 & ISO 14001 Certified Co.,
Regd. Office: 2525/193, 1st Floor, Onkar Nagar-A, Tri Nagar,
Delhi-110035
Ph.: 09350849407, 09312235086
E-mail: info@pendownpress.com
Branch Office: 1A/2A, 20, Hari Sadan, Ansari Road,
Daryaganj, New Delhi-110002
Ph.: 011-45794768
Website: PendownPress.com

First Edition: 2021
Price:
ISBN: 978-93-91266-11-0

Layout Design: Pendown Press Publishing
Printed and bound in India by Thomson Press India Ltd.

CONTENTS

DEDICATED TO...

*My father, late Shri Dev Raj Arya,
my real-life Hero who taught me to appreciate
the value of life, and without whom,
I would not be the person I am.*

THE AUTHOR'S JOURNEY

Hello!

My name is Dr. Rakesh Arya, and I am a scheduling Scientist. Through this book, I am delighted to share with you the essence of my learning from my 35 years of extensive work experience.

I am a B.Com, M.B.A, and a Ph.D. degree holder, and in my wide-spanning career, I have been blessed to have interacted with lacs of people across the world. I have been even more fortunate to have coached thousands of Industrialists and top Corporate Executives globally. This includes people from companies worth thousands of crores and employing more than a thousand people.

My coaching and training programs have been highly successful, benefitting even those who had taken various other prestigious global courses but were disappointed with the results.

I firmly believe that to coach well, you must learn from the best. To this end, I have trained with and worked with the best of the best in the world like T. Harv Eker, Robin Sharma, Tony Robbins, Sam Caw thorn, and Brian Tracy, to name a few.

In my thirst for knowledge to live a fulfilled life, my learning experience has traversed a wide path from the timeless life-altering philosophy of the 'Geeta' to the modern-day management techniques of the Harvard University.

An essential aspect of my learning and growth curve has been my synergy with Mother Nature which has added a mystic and spiritual dimension to my personality, helping me realize my highest potential. For the past many years, I have made sure to travel to the hills every two months to commune with nature. Introspecting in the emerald green ambiance of the hills, becoming one with my surroundings, and pondering on my life and humanity as a collective has brought me to a simple yet profound truth about life.

Life Is Very Easy!

"Let's never, never, never, forget these three things: An easy, fun life is totally achievable. A plan and many steps may be needed. No matter how tired and deep in the mud we are, let's make sure we take one little step forward every day."
–Rodolfo Peon

Popular author Rodolfo Peon has genuinely captured the essence of life and success in these words; my own experience and meditative introspections have led me to a similar truth.

The 'Buddha' realization and truth that my journey inwards has brought to me is; that life is very easy; we complicate things. Life is meant to be lived fully in all its glory with fun, freedom, and fulfillment; even with all its challenges, there is a simple code to cracking life.

Using this code, I have been living my life on my own terms. All areas of my life are in complete harmony, be it professional, personal, emotional, social, or financial. Life for me is **Very Easy.**

Sounds like a miracle??? Well, it actually is! However, it is a miracle that anyone can create.

If I can do it, you can too!

Zero To Hero

Often in the world of cinema, we hear that a particular script was written with a certain Hero in mind, that the writer/director always knew who they wanted as the Hero while developing the project.

Other times it's the complete opposite; the story is written first, with no thought to who the Hero would be. Once the story is ready, then the casting begins, and a suitable Hero/Actor is selected.

In the case of this book, I developed the script first through my life experiences and learnings and then while pondering on how my life had changed due to the script of the Five Golden Rules operating in my life. I realized that we are all always wanting to move from where we are and to reach higher. So since we are not content staying where we are, it would not be wrong to say that we are at point Zero, and the highest point that we want to move to is to rise above everything and become extraordinary. We seek to become Heroes.

This desire to go from Zero to Hero is a universal phenomenon; every person aspires to this, everyone wants to be a Hero.

Also, there is a spiritual aspect to this; the more we understand life, the more we see that those who are genuinely knowledgeable, enlightened, and successful are more humble and grounded. They know that *Neutrality* or *SHOONYA* is the true state of being. That Zero hood is, infact, the other face of Herohood.

Thus whichever way we look at it, either practically or from a metaphysical/spiritual standpoint, our primary endeavor in life is From *ZERO TO HERO*.

So this script was written first, and then the amazing casting was done! YOU, my readers and friends are the *HERO* of this book. Yes! Each one of you, no matter where in life you are, no matter what resources you have at your disposal, using the 5 Golden Rules I have outlined in this book, you will be able to go from Zero to Hero even in a crisis.

THE FIVE GOLDEN RULES

Having combined all my extensive experiences while coaching and learning, having bridged the gap between traditional philosophies and modern techniques to bring the best of both worlds together, and having journeyed inward to the self, I have devised the '5 Golden Rules System' that is practical and easy to implement. This system has changed my life, helping me live life joyfully and successfully on my own terms with complete ease.

Living my life wonderfully, I consider it my moral and social responsibility toward all my fellow travelers on this journey of life to share these 5 Golden rules for them to begin living the life they are meant to, on their terms. So here I am sharing these 5 Golden Rules that are a must for all of us to journey from Zero to Hero!

Become A Legend

Through my own experience, I have realized that the essence of life is encapsulated in these 5 Golden Rules that I will be sharing with you in the coming chapters.

This book though written in these challenging times of the Covid-19 Pandemic, is timeless and evergreen. This book aims to help you in turning your life around 360 degrees. If you are determined to succeed and contribute to the world to create history and become a legend, this book is for you.

If you wish to be the 'Hero' of your life, living not just to exist but to impact this world and mark your presence, then this book is for you.

This book is for everyone irrespective of their circumstances, whether they are good or not-so-good or unfortunate. It does not matter whether you have immense resources or limited resources at your disposal. It does not matter whether you are at point Zero.

Everyone who uses the 5 Must-Have Golden Rules creates the possibility of 'Marking Their Presence' in life as a HERO in Golden Letters.

ACKNOWLEDGEMENTS

To begin with, I would like to express my gratitude to my mother, without whose blessings this book would not have been written. I also owe huge thanks to my wife and my son for their unstinted support and for generously loaning me the time that belonged to them to write this book.

I also wish to thank my team for supporting me so that I was free to write this book without any distractions.

I also want to take this opportunity to extend my immense gratitude to my coach and consultant, Mr. Akshar Yadav, for inspiring me and guiding me at every juncture. Last but definitely not least, sincere thanks to my brother and publisher, Dinesh Verma, for encouraging me and personally supporting me through the entire process.

THE 2 TYPES OF PEOPLE

THE MISSING

While interacting with people at my coaching/training sessions and programs, as well as socially, I find that a lot of people are struggling to shift their lives into a higher gear. Most people want more out of their lives than they currently have. Innumerable people come to me for advice on how to succeed in life, and I tell them that no matter what the circumstances, no matter how crushed you are in life, you can always bounce back.

*Even if you are at point Zero,
it is possible to go from ZERO TO HERO!*

The key to a successful life is:

Knowing what to do and doing it!

Though various researches and theories propound different types of personalities dividing people based on their personal traits, some ideas suggest four personality types; others organize people into sixteen personality types.

However, from all my interactions with people who are missing the joy in life or unendingly waiting for success to knock on their door, I can safely say that they can be divided into two kinds of people:

*The Type 1 People; Something Is Missing In Life
(Zindagi Me Kuch Maza Nahin Aa Raha)*

> *"We must have a theme, a goal, a purpose in our lives. If you don't know where you're aiming, you don't have a goal."*
> **–Mary Kay Ash**

The first kinds of people are those who have been blessed with everything in life, a good career, a happy family, social respect, money, etc., yet these people do not feel fulfilled; discontent keeps nagging at them repeatedly. On the face of it, they have no reason to be unhappy, yet they do not feel completely happy. They are unable to enjoy life fully.

What these people are missing in their lives is a Purposeful Goal; they need a purpose to inspire them and infuse more passion and excitement in their lives. They need to identify something more significant and meaningful in life than what they are currently doing. No amount of money or even the most beautiful relationship can make up for not having a 'Passion of Purpose' in one's life.

Mary Kay Ash, the multi-millionaire American businesswoman and founder of Mary Kay Cosmetics, said it best, as have many others, that:

A life without purpose is a lost life!

My only advice to these people is that if you wish to live a life of joy, meaning, and fulfillment, it is essential to identify that one Passionate Purpose in your life and then build your life around it.

A great example to study here would be self-made millionaire Timothy Kim, host of the financial blog *TubofCash.com*.

Having made successful investments in the stock market since the age of 19. He started out with just $500 in his name, and at 31, he became a millionaire. Kim has everything in life; he has money and fame, he is healthy, and his personal life is fine. **YET KIM IS BORED and UNFULFILLED!**

Why????

Here is the answer in his own words:

> *"Most people want to add value to society."*
> –Timothy Kim

He desires to do something for society, to find meaning and purpose in life, something bigger than just his own happiness.

Therefore, to be truly happy, it is essential to have a purpose more significant than just our selfish desires.

The Type 2 People; Nothing Is Working In Life
(Kuchh Bhi Kaam Nhin Ban Raha)

> *"The path to success is to take massive, determined actions."*
> –Tony Robbins

The second kinds of people are those who constantly complain that they work hard, put in a lot of effort, and have tried everything, but nothing seems to work. They feel that success eludes them despite their best efforts. These people never take responsibility for their own failure/results; instead, they always squarely blame other people or circumstances.

Nothing is happening in their lives, and success eludes these people constantly because they are not taking targeted or focused action; instead, they are scattering their energy all over the place and spreading themselves thin. They think and plan much more than they do. However, thoughts, unless translated into action, are meaningless.

What these people need to do is decide what they want and take action on their goals. Only then will things start happening and working in their life. The simple equation to succeed in life is:

DECIDING + DOING = HAPPENING

As discussed, deciding on what you want and taking determined action toward it is the only way to succeed. Simply deciding on what we want and planning out ways to achieve it will not help us achieve our purpose or goals. Unless the intention is manifested as action, it is of no good.

> *"What we think or what we know or what we believe is, in the end, of little consequence. The only consequence is what we do."*
> **– John Ruskin**

Such people often get stuck in "Analysis Paralysis," trying to make their plan perfect instead of taking action. The window of opportunity then passes them by, and they are left complaining that nothing ever works out for them even though they work hard.

In an era when information is often just two clicks away, "Analysis Paralysis" can be the undoing of your plans. Thus once you have prepared sufficiently, make sure to take action.

So first decide what you want and then don't sit on that idea, don't procrastinate, make that goal a reality, take action, and make it happen otherwise, as famous American businessman Arnold Glasow says:

> *"An idea not coupled with action will never get any bigger than the brain cell it occupied."*
> **–Arnold Glasow**

These types of people are often masters of Procrastination and keep shying away from focused action. Procrastination is one of the main barriers blocking you from getting up, making the right decisions, and living the dream life you've thought of.

These procrastinators keep blaming people and circumstances for their inaction and keep waiting for the perfect moment or perfect circumstances.

Sometimes all our opportunities seem to be at our fingertips, but we can't seem to reach them.

These people also tend to blame others and circumstances for their results or lack of them instead of taking responsibility for their lives, reviewing their actions honestly, and then modifying them.

> *"The victim mindset dilutes the human potential.*
> *By not accepting personal responsibility*
> *for our circumstances, we greatly reduce*
> *our power to change them."*
> **–Steve Maraboli**

Taking personal responsibility for all the things in our life, the good, the bad, and the ugly, is one of the most empowering things you can do. Only then can you shape your future.

The words Response and Ability are inherent in the word Responsibility. That means you have the ability to choose your response to whatever happens mindfully. Viktor E. Frankl has beautifully summarized this:

> *"Between stimulus and response, there is space.*
> *In that space is our power to choose our response.*
> *In our response lies our growth and our freedom."*
> **–Viktor E. Frankl**

The third thing that these kinds of people do is spreading themselves thin and scattering their energy instead of focusing on their goals without distraction.

There are tons of things lying in wait to distract you from your ultimate goal. However, in every success story, the longest and hardest chapter is the one about determination. Our success depends on many things, but focus, willpower, and determination top the charts. Many people believe that we are born with determination and those that succeed are simply the fortunate ones born with an abundant supply. That, however, is very far from the truth. It is not merely luck that helps others succeed and the lack of it that makes you fail. Ask any successful person. They will tell you they were not born with more determination; they always found a way to harness and use what they have more effectively. Focus and determination are qualities that can be cultivated and will lead you to success faster than waiting and hoping for Lady Luck to smile on you.

> *Don't be either of these types of people, instead take responsibility for your life, find your purpose set your goal and take action toward it, and you will be well on your way to success and becoming a HERO!*

CHAPTER 2

THE HEROES

Hero; a person who is admired for their courage, outstanding achievements, or noble qualities.

This is how the dictionary defines a Hero.

Heroes are larger than life. They inspire us, and they give us hope; they are beacons of light when all is dark, and they instill in us the courage to push our boundaries & scale summits.

We all want to be Heroes in life.

Which one of us hasn't grown up on tales of Superheroes? Be it through books, through our grandparents, or cinema and Television, tales of glorious heroes, leave us enraptured. Books and cinema have immortalized various kinds of heroes for us that we have idolized throughout generations. A hero is an integral part of any and every story, be it an art-house film, a commercial film, a comedy, or a thriller; no tale is complete without the main protagonist, the Hero.

Heroes are always of 2 kinds:

THE TYPE 1; A HERO IS BORN!

> *"You are stronger than you believe.*
> *You have greater powers than you know."*
> – Antiope to Diana, Wonder Woman movie

These types of heroes are born with special powers right from the beginning. They begin to exhibit uniqueness right from the early stages of their life, and people are in awe of them. They carry an aura of magic around them. Sometimes their heroic powers can even be fear-inducing. However, they all have one thing in common; they all exhibit some extraordinary traits from birth or early childhood.

The most excellent example of a hero with the power born would be '**Lord Krishna**'. He showed his abilities right from day one by controlling the ebbing and flowing of the waters of the Yamuna when it wanted to worship his feet and after that by killing various demons effortlessly while still in the crib.

There are numerous other examples of heroes born with their powers, like **Thor, Aquaman,** our very own **Bahubali** who showed incredible strength from babyhood, and our beloved **Krrish,** who had such chart-busting mental abilities that his grandmother had to take him into hiding for his protection.

Then, there is the inimitable **Wonder Woman,** who was born with incredible strength, speed, and self-healing powers. These Heroes may hone their ability even more in their lifetimes, but the bottom line is that they are born with these powers. **They are born unique.**

There are numerous examples of Heroes in various fields of life who showed uncommon ability right since childhood.

The legendary Music Composer Mozart began playing music on his harpsichord at age 4 and began composing music at the age of 5. At 7 years old, he was already touring to showcase his musical abilities. In addition to his phenomenal musical abilities, Mozart was also gifted with a remarkable memory. He could hear pieces of music as long as 12-15 minutes and commit them to memory without needing to follow written sheets.

Juana Ines De La Cruz, one of the most famous Mexican writers of the baroque times, showed remarkable intellect since early childhood and, despite her circumstances, could read fluently at age 3 without being taught. As a child, she mastered Latin in just 20 lessons; at age 16, she was quizzed by 40 professors from various fields of knowledge in the Court of the Viceroy of New Spain. She astounded them all with the brilliance and depth of her knowledge without being fazed.

Famous Mathematician Srinivasa Ramanujam is another such example, he showed incredible mathematical acumen since childhood and was completely self-taught till the age of 16, yet he went on to become legendary, even being elected a Fellow of the Royal Societ in 1918.

Judit Polgar the Chess Prodigy showed incredible abilities as a child and went on to become a real Hero; she became the only woman to be ranked in the top 10 of all-time greats of Chess irrespective of gender. She was also the youngest Grand Master ever at the age of 15.

World-famous musician/singer Stevie Wonder demonstrated prodigal musical talent since childhood despite being blind. He began recording and performing professionally even before hitting his teenage years at the tender age of 12.

THE TYPE 2; A HERO IS MADE!

> *"A hero is an ordinary individual who finds the strength to persevere and endure in spite of overwhelming obstacles."*
> – Christopher Reeve

The second type of Heroes are those who are not born with any special powers; instead, it is the reverse. These people are born into unfortunate circumstances like poverty, disease, abuse, disability, discrimination, etc., and continue facing it for a larger part of life. However, against all the odds, they rise above all these challenges to come out victorious.

There are innumerable examples of this category of heroes in folklore, cinema, and even in real life. Though born special, he was unaware of his magic; Harry Potter the Boy Wonder would be a perfect example of this category, orphaned at a young age and brought up by abusive and discriminatory relatives. The boy wonder went on to vanquish a strong villain becoming a memorable Hero.

Closer home, any of Mr. Amitabh Bachchan's iconic characters in Deewar, Laawaris, or Trishul are great examples of this type of Hero. In all these films, the Hero fights injustice and builds a great life for himself despite poverty, abuse, betrayal, oppression, and discrimination.

Despite being deaf and blind since the age of 19 months, Helen Keller went on to read, write and speak. She became the first deaf-blind person to earn a Bachelor of Arts Degree and was a prolific author who went on to write 14 books.

Martin Luther King Jr, despite continued racial discrimination and harassment by authorities, worked tirelessly for the Civil Rights Movement and went on to win the Nobel Peace Prize for his contribution.

Oprah Winfrey, the queen of Television, was born into abject poverty to a teenaged single mother. She was molested in childhood and her teens; she then became pregnant at 14. Her son was born prematurely and died in infancy. Yet against all the odds, she became a Co-Anchor on a Radio show at 19, and then, of course, as we all know, she went on to have the highest-rated T.V show in that category. A show that was syndicated for straight 25 years. She was the wealthiest African-American of the 20th century and America's first Black Multi-Billionaire. She is a Hero and role model to all those who battle oppression and adversity and is one of the most prominent philanthropists of our times.

Michael Phelps, the legendary swimmer, suffered from ADHD as a child and was also on medication for it for some time. People with ADHD suffer from restlessness, impulsiveness, and a very short attention span. Yet Michael was determined and dedicated to his sport and was hyper focused on swimming,an activity that he is passionate about. By channeling his energy and Focus, he has been able to exploit the positive side of ADHD. Even in the face of the challenge, this single-minded Focus has led Michael to win 8 Gold Medals in just 1 Olympic alone. He also has a record of 19 Olympic Medals, out of which 15 are Gold.

Miss India Manya Singh exemplifies this category of heroism in recent times. She battled poverty, prejudice, and patriarchy to reach the pinnacle of success. Born to an Auto Rickshaw driver from a small town, she had no formal schooling, yet she taught herself many skills and studied long distance to become a beacon of light and motivation to a whole generation of young Indians. She taught us never to give up on our dreams.

All these amazing people are examples of this type of Heroes in real life. They overcame extreme victimization, discrimination, disability, and disease to become role models for many generations imparting hope, courage, and dignity to countless people.

CHAPTER 3

WHAT DRIVES THE HERO

Now that we understand the glory and courage of Heroes and also the two types of Heroes, it surely makes us wonder what drives these Heroes to take on the world and emerge victorious even in death-defying situations.

Though Heroes are of two kinds, their driving force is the same. What drives these Heroes are their dreams and desires.

DREAMS AND DESIRES

> *"Hold fast to dreams, for if dreams die,*
> *life is a broken-winged bird that cannot fly."*
> –Langston Hughes

> *"Desire is the starting point of all achievement,*
> *not a hope, not a wish, but a keen pulsating*
> *desire which transcends everything."*
> –Napoleon Hill

What fuels Heroes are their dreams and desires. It is these dreams that don't let them sit idle, instead egging them on to action. Desires are the fuel of life; if people had no desires to work toward or look forward to, they wouldn't be living at all. The fulfillment of dreams and desires is the reason for living.

So are these dreams and desires different for different kinds of Heroes?

No! The dreams and desires that fuel Heroes are universal. At the crux of all dreams and desires is any one or a combination of the following underlying reasons. This holds true for any Hero and any dream or desire that they have.

1. To WIN something or someone!

2. To ACHIEVE a goal!

3. To STOP something or someone!

Winner Takes It All

> *"Winning isn't everything;*
> *it's the only thing."*
> –Vince Lombardi

Legendary football coach Vince Lombardi said winning is everything. That is the case with these kinds of Heroes. The first reason that drives a Hero is the desire to Win. In folklore and mythology, there are countless tales where a Hero is born out of their journey to win back something they have lost or their parents or ancestors have lost. They could also be on a mission to win back something society has lost collectively. It could be a kingdom, a treasure, a competition, the hand of a beloved,the love of their chosen one, a job, or just their dignity.

Apt examples of this would be Mr. Bachchan as Vijay in the blockbuster Trishul, who wants to win back his mother's dignity and his legitimacy as a child, Mr. Bachchan again in the box office hit Baghban winning back his and his wife's dignity, togetherness, and financial stability after losing it all to the greedy machinations of his sons. Another great example close home is the Hero Mahendra, aka Bahubali, who fights to win back his mother's dignity and sanity as well as his erstwhile kingdom. Chak De India is also a great example where Kabir Khan loses everything, glory, money, and, worst of all, his dignity, but he wins it all back.

Venturing into Hollywood, we also have examples of acclaimed films like 'The Pursuit Of Happiness' and 'Jerry Maguire' where the Heroes put it all back together and win after losing everything. 'The Shaw shank Redemption,' one of the most iconic movies of all time, has the protagonist winning back his freedom after years of being wrongly imprisoned.

Not just in reel life, in real life, too, there is no dearth of such winning heroes. Vinod Bansal, the famous Bansal Coaching classes pioneer, lost his job and fell prey to Muscular Dystrophy. Yet, he went on to win back his wealth and respectability by creating the nationwide Bansal Coaching that began with just eight students in Kota. Mr. Amitabh Bachchan is a Hero in real life too. After losing everything with ABCL and running up huge debts, he worked hard to bounce back with even more net worth and fame.

The Goal Is Worth Achieving

> *"It took me 17 years & 114 days to become an overnight success"*
> **– Lionel Messi**

The second kind of Heroes are those who are driven by a goal. That is all they think about, dream about, and desire. They live and breathe that goal. Sometimes they are conditioned toward the achievement of that goal from childhood itself.

This kind of Hero is determined to achieve something, and they tirelessly keep working toward it despite various forms of failure, rejection, and other challenges. They do not take no for an answer.

A great example of a Hero focused on achieving their goals is Bhuvan in Lagaan, who overcomes all challenges to win the game against the British.

Also, real & reel life Hero Mahavir Singh Phogat who was popularized through the film Dangal is one such Hero who was focused on training his daughters to win medals for India in wrestling.

Thomas Alva Edison failed in 1000 experiments but did not lose Focus and went on to invent the Light Bulb and many other important inventions. Twelve publishers rejected celebrity author J.K Rowling for her Harry Potter series, but she did not give up, and today that series has made her a world-famous multi-millionaire. Walt Disney was fired from his newspaper job for not being creative enough, yet he never gave up on his dreams and created an empire and history, winning a record 22 Oscars. Michael Jordan, the ace Basketball player, was kicked out of his school Basketball team in his sophomore year, but he kept going and became one of the world's most sought-after players.

Crusading For A Better World

> *"Injustice anywhere is a threat to justice everywhere."*
> – Martin Luther King Jr.

The third driving force behind a Hero is their desire to stop someone wreaking havoc in their own lives or on a larger community. It could also be the desire to fight against some wrong or injustice toward the self or society.

The number of Heroes who emerge from fighting injustice is huge. Be it in books, folklore, Television, or cinema. Marvel and D.C., the two biggest comic and movie houses, have built a whole industry around Heroes who fight injustice and stop Super-Villains from destroying the planet.

The Boy Wonder Harry Potter is a glowing example of this genre;he was born to stop the evil Voldemort's terror.

Lord Krishna was a prime example of this kind of Hero; he was born to fight against Evil.

Spiderman, Superman, Batman, Ironman, and Wonder Woman are all heroes fighting injustices and stopping villains from destroying the planet.

In real life, famous leaders like Mahatma Gandhi, Nelson Mandela, Martin Luther King, Baba Amte, Anna Hazare, etc., were Heroes who fought to stop various social injustices.

A SPANNER IN THE WHEELS

*"The greater the obstacle,
the more glory in overcoming it."*
– Molière

Like an electrocardiogram (ECG), life is never a straight line. Life keeps throwing curve balls, and Heroes are no exception to this rule. Whenever a Hero is well on their way to their mission, something happens out of the blue to throw them offtrack. The universe always throws a spanner in the works for Heroes. These unexpected challenges upset the balance and derail the heroes for some time, yet they make them even more determined to reach their goals.

These obstacles, hurdles, or spanners are generally of three types:

1. **Love is in the air; Attraction becomes a distraction:** Love and attraction can be one of the reasons a Hero goes off-track. On their way to achieving their goal, the Hero sometimes falls in love or suddenly becomes attracted to someone. Sometimes the one they are attracted to could even be from the enemy camp. The desire to build a beautiful life together with their beloved or at the very least spend time with them can prove distracting to their success.

   An example would be Salman Khan as Tiger in the blockbuster Ek Tha Tiger falling in love with Katrina Kaif's character, and he is distracted for a while. Still, ultimately his patriotism finds a way to balance his personal and professional lives.

2. **Out of the blue Emergencies:** Sometimes a Hero's mission is derailed because of sudden emergencies that could be in any form and unexpected. It could be the breakdown of machinery that is critical to the success of the mission. A family member could fall ill, a pandemic could break out, and the Hero could lose a loved one or could suddenly lose their money or power. Any of these situations would be a major setback to the Hero and their dreams and desires. In the movie Tere Naam, Salman Khan is well on his way to a smooth life with his beloved and his small happy family after turning over a new leaf, but suddenly he sees a disabled girl being molested, stepping in to save her his whole life is thrown off-track.

3. **Personal setbacks Mental/Physical:** Many times a Hero's journey receives a massive setback because of extremely personal tragedies. Sudden mental or emotional pain and debilitating physical illness can cause upheaval in a hero's life. However, these setbacks are always temporary. A true Hero always manages to turn challenges into opportunities and comes out victorious.

   A case in point could be Ghajini. Aamir Khan suffers from short-term memory loss due to extreme physical torture and deep psychological pain but ends up demolishing the villain.

   Another apt example is Dr. Strange, the iconic superhero character who became crippled but managed to channel superpowers with his mind.

A Hero and their challenges are inseparable, but the bigger the obstacles, the bigger the glory. Heroes keep rising in the face of challenges; like the legendary phoenix, they keep rising from the ashes and keep soaring higher and higher.

CHAPTER 5

THE 3 Cs OF LIFE

Understanding the value of the 3 Fs and working toward them is one thing. Achieving them is another thing; on the path to the 3Fs lie the 3 Cs that are waiting to pounce upon you and drive you off track at every opportunity.

These 3 Cs can sometimes be very sneaky, creeping up on you suddenly, or sometimes they can be right in your face. These debilitating 3 Cs are:

- Circumstances
- Confusion
- Crowd

CIRCUMSTANCES

> *"Circumstances do not make the man; they reveal him."*
> – James Allen

Who among us hasn't fallen prey to circumstances. They have the power to make or break us. Imagine a bright young student dedicatedly working toward their goal of getting a degree from the most prestigious university in the world. They already come from an economically weaker background, but somehow their parents manage to fund their studies. Suddenly, the father loses his job and can no longer afford that university even though admission has been granted. Now the student could succumb to circumstances, give up on their dream, or meet up with university authorities, other business houses, NGOs or friends, and extended family to support their education.

Other examples could be falling sick or having an accident on the day of a life-changing event. Etc.

CONFUSION

> *"Life is full of confusion. Confusion of love, passion, and romance. Confusion of family and friends. Confusion with life itself. What path we take, what turns we make. How we roll our dice."*
> – Matthew Underwood

American actor Matthew Underwood has summarized the confusion we all face at various junctures of life. We are surrounded by options and burdened by conflicting expectations and advice. Reconciling our true desires and aptitude with the expectations of others becomes tough.

CROWD

> *"Those who follow the crowd usually get lost in it."*
> – Rick Warren

Crowd or herd mentality is another serious detriment to living a fulfilled life. It is always stopping us from finding our purpose; everyone is expected to follow the beaten path. Anyone who dares to walk their own path is mostly discouraged. We are always expected to blend into the crowd. For example, we are all forced to focus only on academics even though our true aptitude may lie in the arts or sports. Even today, parents force their children to follow the traditional occupations of engineering and medicine even though the number of unemployed doctors and engineers is at an all-time high. They shy away from letting their children go into other professions like art, writing, music, sports, etc.

Staying true to one's identity and having the courage not blindly to follow the crowd is no mean task.

CHAPTER 6

THE 3 Fs OF LIFE

To be a Hero in life, it is essential to understand that an easy life is based on 3 things. We may need each of these elements or need all three together; however, it is primarily the interplay of all these three elements that make life worth living.

The best example of this is small children; they are free and not bound by any shackles and do not filter their sentiments to fit society's expectations; they are having fun with their lives, smiles, and laughter unadulterated, and they are fulfilled by their fun and freedom.

That is why it is always necessary to keep the child within us alive.

- Fun
- Freedom
- Fulfillment

Let's dig a little deeper into each of these cornerstones of a meaningful life.

FUN

> *"If it's not fun, you're not doing it right."*
> – Bob Basso

Fun is a small 3 letter word that has a massive impact on the quality of life. No matter the amount of money or success we have, we will never be happy if we are not enjoying it, so everyone craves fun. That is why the proverb; all work and no play, makes Jack a dull boy. Entertainment and recreation are important to have fun, but it is also important to enjoy what we do to have fun. It is, therefore, important to be clear about what we genuinely want to do and then pursue it.

For example, If a person interested in the arts is forced to be an engineer due to financial and societal expectations will never have fun, no matter how successful they may be.

FREEDOM

> *"Freedom lies in being bold."*
> – Robert Frost

Freedom is our default state of being; it is the ability to think, express, and act as per our desires without harming another. But as we grow up, we succumb to society's expectations and norms and lose our inherent personality. We feel trapped in this existence. Athome, freedom could mean the allowance to be one's true self in front of parents, siblings, spouse, or children. At work, it is having an environment that shapes and encourages your skills and creative ideas to flourish. It is the right to choose your political and social views and beliefs and act accordingly in society.

Continuing with the above example of the Artist forced to be an engineer, they will never be happy as their freedom of choice has been curbed. Another example could be of a couple where one partner is an extrovert and wants to go out and party every weekend, while the other wishes to just chill at home with a good book or a movie. Yet when either of them is forced to behave as per the other's wish continually, their freedom of self is compromised and could lead to a rocky relation.

FULFILLMENT

> *"Only those who have learned the power of sincere and selfless contribution experience life's deepest joy: true fulfillment."*
> – Tony Robbins

Fulfillment is a result of the above two elements mostly. One can only have fun when one is free to choose because then they will choose the career, relationship, or social activity that gives the most joy, so freedom and fun can lead to fulfillment as the sense of purpose is achieved when you have the freedom to be in the right place at the right time.

Fulfillment is the sense of joy that is bigger than the self, which comes from setting and achieving goals that are way out of your comfort zone and aligned with a bigger purpose than just serving yourself.

Thus the 3 Fs Fun, Freedom, and Fulfillment are the cornerstones of life and are responsible for catapulting an ordinary person to the status of a Hero.

CHAPTER 7

THE 5 GOLDEN RULES EVERY HERO NEEDS

Finally, having understood how Heros work and the challenges that they face in life and having discussed that life can be easy if we know how to live it, we come to the last part of this book.

You are now ready to receive the 5 Golden rule system that I have personally used to live the life that I want with complete harmony, balance, and joy. These rules will help you enhance productivity with limited resources in critical times.

Though very simple in nature, these rules are genuinely golden if followed with dedication and applied to all areas of life.

They are simple, philosophical yet practical, and easy to use. They are:

- Clarity
- Focus
- Writing
- Serious Scheduling
- Evaluation

CLARITY

> *"There are few things more powerful than a life lived with passionate clarity."*
> – Erwin McManus

As discussed, confusion is one of the biggest enemies of success and productivity. If your mind is hazy and bogged down with confusion, it isn't easy to have a direction and be focused on your goals.

Without a clear mindset, it's easy to spread yourself thin by scattering your energy and then feel frustrated and talk yourself out of pursuing your goals.

It is crucial to identify and be clear about your purpose/ goals and then work toward them accordingly. Let's take a small example:

When you visit a restaurant, and you are in the mood to eat a burger, what do you do? Imagine being confused and asking your server to get you something warm and round with a filling inside of vegetables… now, the results could be hilarious; you could end up with a vadapav, a stuffed parantha, or a burger if you are lucky.

However, if you order a burger, you can sit back and be sure that you will receive a burger.

So the first and most essential step to achieving what you want is being clear about what you want.

- Clarity leads to Focus and direction
- Clarity helps smoothen and organize your efforts
- Clarity helps you to prioritize
- Clarity helps combat self-doubt

Focus

> *"Always remember, your focus determines your reality."*
> – George Lucas

Once you have complete clarity on what you want to achieve and are clear about your dreams and desires, the next step on the path to success is staying focused on your goals and actions. When you are focused, nothing can stop you from achieving your dreams and desires.

Focused people make a plan and stick to it. They work on their goals every single day, no matter what the distractions.

George Lucas is the billionaire genius behind the epic Star Wars franchise. He focused single-mindedly on his desire to create this series. It took him many years to bring it into reality, but he never lost sight of his goal, and the rest, as they say, is history. By staying focused on his work, he created an incredible reality and is an icon and pioneer in this genre.

Staying focused consistently on your goals is hard. In the beginning, we're highly motivated; that motivation wanes over time. We get caught up in other things;we get stuck and frustrated, overloaded, overworked, distracted, and get derailed from our track.

The following three golden rules will ensure that you stay focused and achieve your dreams and desires.

WRITE IT DOWN

> *"Write it down. Written goals have a way of transforming wishes into wants, cant's into cans; dreams into plans, and plans into reality. Don't just think it-ink it!"*
> — **Michael Korda**

Once you are clear about what you want and are focused on your goals, writing them down instead of just having them as vague thoughts in your mind will help you stay focused on them.

If you haven't written out your goals, then you're bypassing the essential part of the road to success.

When you don't write your goals, they stay in the abstract. They're less tangible, even if you think they're as real as they can be. Writing them down makes them clear and specific. It gives them a life of their own. It infuses into them a positive energy and reaffirms them.

If your dreams and desires are not committed to paper, it is easy to lose sight of them. Think about it this way, If you can not even make an effort to write them down, what are the chances of you achieving them.

If you have them written down, you can keep visiting them often and visualizing them for faster success. This will help you stay focused and take action toward achieving them.

SERIOUS SCHEDULING

"The rich fruit of spontaneity grows in the garden that is well tended by the discipline of schedule."
– John Piper

Scheduling is the art of planning activities to achieve your goals and priorities in the time available to you. Once you are clear and focused on your efforts, it's vital to layout a floor plan for the what's, the how's, the why's, and the when's.

Your actions just cannot be haywire and taken whenever it suits your whims and fancies. Instead, they have to be detailed in a precise manner and time. This is what Scheduling is about.

However, we are not just talking about Scheduling here. We are talking about 'Serious Scheduling'. There's a vital difference between the two.

Scheduling is simply about setting aside time for something.

Serious Scheduling is about sticking to that commitment.

Let me elaborate on Serious Scheduling for you simply:

When it is your wedding day, or an operation at the hospital, or an important interview, or a critical flight to catch, do you take it for granted??? No!

You are alert and make sure to be at the venue on time. You make all the efforts and precautions needed to stick to that schedule. This is Serious Scheduling. The prioritizing and the commitment makes all the difference.

It's essential to stick to the scheduled action plan to achieve your dreams and desires with this same commitment.

EVALUATION

> *"Think about your goals and review them daily.*
> *Every morning when you begin, take action on*
> *the most important task you can accomplish*
> *to achieve your most important goal*
> *at the moment."*
> *– Brian Tracy*

The 5th and final golden rule is evaluation. As you work toward your dreams and desires, it is crucial to evaluate and review your efforts; you must check and analyze whether or not they're working to get you what you want. Are your actions moving you toward success? If not, why not? What can you tweak, change, or get rid of to make them work?

You can set up an evaluation plan, break down your action plans into milestones, and review them accordingly. You can have quarterly, monthly, or weekly evaluation plans as per your need. However, it helps to have mini-evaluations daily to make sure that no efforts are wasted along the way.

When evaluating and reviewing, make sure you set aside a specific time for it and give it the attention and consideration it deserves. Also, while evaluating and examining your efforts, it is necessary to be fair and honest. 'Look at the results Objectively.

Don't underplay your achievements, and don't sugarcoat your shortfalls.

Be honest and flexible, after reviewing tweak and change what is not working. This way, your efforts are guaranteed to bring results.

Now I have given you:

"The 5 Golden Rules For Enhancing Productivity With Limited Resources In Critical Time"

The ball is in your court now; take charge of your life, become a Hero and live life easily and harmoniously with success and joy!

- It does not matter what your circumstances are.

- It does not matter whether you have an abundance of resources or you have limited resources.

- It does not matter whether it is these critical and challenging times of the pandemic.

Dear reader, using these 5 Golden rules, you can begin your journey to leading a fulfilling life right now.

Through this book, you have got everything a person needs to become a HERO!

I would be delighted to be an even more significant part of your journey to success.

Imagine how wonderful it would be if you and I could spend an hour together and experience the energies of possibility live.

If you truly want to live this book at supersonic speed with an advanced tool to give wings to your destiny, I invite you to connect with me for an hour-long "Intenese Value Condensed Zero To Hero Workshop."

This workshop is normally priced at INR 10,000.00; however, for you, my readers, if you register through this link right away, it is only INR 499.00!

Your heroic dream life is only a click away... Register now!!!

https://imjo.in/CK3bsm

Let's embark on a new journey of success, joy, and abundance.

Wishing you a Golden Heroic Life

Yours sincerely

Dr. Rakesh Arya

EMBRACING YOUR PURPOSE

> *"There's no greater gift than to honor your life's calling. It's why you were born. And how you become most truly alive."*
> – Oprah Winfrey

A purpose not only adds meaning to life, but it also imbues it with innumerable other benefits such as:

Purpose Facilitates Focus

Once you discover your life's purpose, it becomes easier to focus on that goal instead of straying into various distractions.

Purpose Facilitates Clarity

People who don't know their purpose in life are not clear about what they want and waste their time on futile things. People who know their purpose in life are unstoppable because they have a direction and Focus. They are clear about their goals.

Purpose Generates Passion

No amount of planning can help you achieve your goals unless you are fuelled by passion. Knowing your purpose enables you to find your true passion, and passion becomes a vital driver for you to achieve something extraordinary. Whether it is a childhood dream or a newly adopted lifestyle, the passion will push you to reach your goals. The passion is what separates those who suffer from Monday Morning Blues from those who can't wait to get back into action at the beginning of the week.

Purpose Magnifies Your Impact

When you have a purpose in life, you express it constantly and base your decisions, thoughts, feelings, and actions around that passionate purpose; you tend to make a greater impact through your work. This encourages a feeling of gratification and keeps you energized to keep going.

Purpose Enables Values and Integrity

With purpose come values, which are an integral aspect of a person's life. Values are the rules that guide our decisions in life and help define our goals. They help us find and connect with others who share our way of viewing the world to form our tribe to magnify our impact. Knowing your purpose in life also helps you live life with integrity because when you identify your purpose, you begin to be true to your values.

Purpose Invites Divine Grace into Your Life

People who know their purpose report a surprising increase in synchronicity and serendipity in their lives. With all this comes a deepening of trust and faith in other people, and they begin to view themselves not in isolation but as integral parts of the entire cosmos. Purpose infuses an element of grace in your life. People who find their purpose tend to live in the flow of the universal stream of consciousness and feel supported by the universe at all times in the most surprising ways. Opportunities seem to knock on your door of their own accord.

Purpose Makes Life Fun & Playful

When you are working toward your goals with the passion of purpose, work becomes play as you begin to enjoy every minute of it. They are able to take pleasure in living a purpose-driven life and are better at tackling every situation in a creative way. Even the dullest thing becomes beautiful and creative when you're motivated by purpose.

The benefits of living a purpose-driven life are innumerable. Living with purpose, you spark positivity and joy, leading you to new opportunities.

You begin to attract and draw in your tribe. Your relationships are also affected in a positive way when you live life with purpose. You seek out new relationships, nurture the existing ones, and build stronger connections with the people around you. You become more helpful to the people around you and in the community as well. You become a role model and begin to make a difference in people's lives.

It is necessary to find and commit to your purpose to lead a fulfilled life, so take the first step to identify your purpose. German poet Johann Wolfgang Von Goethe has said it beautifully:

> *"Until one is committed, there is hesitancy,
> the chance to draw back, always
> ineffectiveness."*
> – Johann Wolfgang Von Goethe

When you commit to living your life with a purpose, amazing things can happen.

PRAISES

"Dr. Rakesh Arya's new book is a short, practical book about the qualities of everyday heroes. He shares life-lessons that will help you build a life worthy of honor and respect. Give a try, read this book... you will also discover True Hero inside you."

– Akshar Yadav
International Marketing Strategist

"Dr. Rakesh Arya, has been one of rarest human being I know on this planet, who is unstoppable in learning and Inspiring people further. This book 'Zero to Hero' written by him, is live example of his own journey and now anyone can become hero from where ever he or she is with 5 Golden basic but divine rules. This book will make you focussed, resilient & habitual of winning."

– Ram Verma
India's number one NLP coach

"A complete game-changer! This book will empower you with a toolkit to bring out the HERO within you and come out victorious in every crisis of your life."

– Dinesh Verma
CEO, Pendown Press

"My experience with author Rakesh Arya has been really really profound. The level of commitments and dedication that I have seen in his personality is remarkable. The book, ZERO to HERO is one of the game- changers, which I believe will set you on to a journey of exploring yourself. Even if you are not a born HERO, we all have a hidden HERO with in us. This book will give you the key to unlock that hidden self where you carry the potential of the entire universe within your soul. It's a must read, I would highly recommend this book for all the people who are looking for a great break through in their life. Rakesh Arya himself, is a real HERO."

– Dr Ramon Llamba
International Celebrity Life coach